I'm the best. I just haven't played yet.

MUHAMMAD ALI, ON HIS GOLF GAME

PRIDE: A SLIPPERY SLOPE

Don't allow pride to short-change you on the golf course or in other areas of life. Admitting our weakness and acknowledging that we need help is usually the first step to renewed hope.

WHEN PRIDE COMETH, THEN COMETH SHAME:
BUT WITH THE LOWLY IS WISDOM.

PROVERBS 11:2

The reason the pro tells you to keep

your head down is so you can't see him laughing.

PHYLLIS DILLER, ENTERTAINER

KEEP AT IT

Perseverance will never be popular, but it is still the price of perfection. Don't give up just because you fail, or give in to some secret habit or sin. Keep striving against it, keep looking to the Lord for help, and He will bring you out of the mess. It may take some time, but you will not go down, but through.

AND LET US NOT BE WEARY IN WELL DOING:
FOR IN DUE SEASON WE SHALL REAP, IF WE FAINT NOT.

GALATIANS 6:9

Golf is a good walk spoiled.

MARK TWAIN, 1835–1910

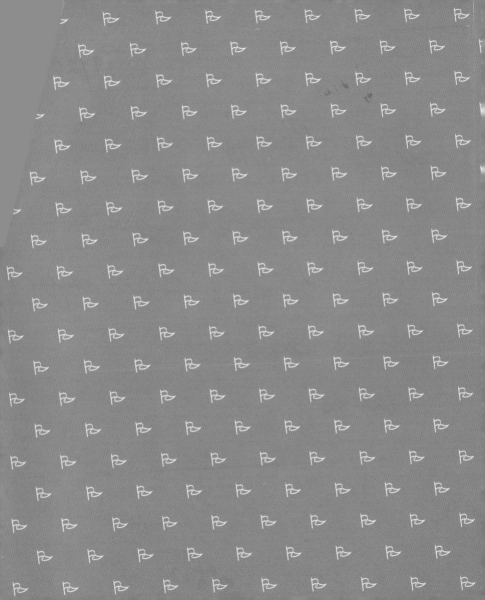

11/1

Dear Kevin,

We wish you a very Happy Birthday and God's Blessings always.

Love Always,
Grammie & Pop
XO

Golf is not my god.

Golf is a game. Jesus Christ is my God.

PAUL AZINGER

GOLF IS A GREAT GAME——BUT IT'S IMPORTANT TO KEEP IT IN PERSPECTIVE. GOLF CAN BE FUN, CHALLENGING, EVEN EXHILARATING; BUT IT CAN ALSO BE FRUSTRATING AND EXASPERATING. WHATEVER YOUR BASIC TEMPERAMENT, GOLF CAN BRING OUT THE NEGATIVE SIDE OF YOUR PERSONALITY. THAT'S WHY WE'VE DESIGNED THIS BOOK: TO HELP YOU FOCUS YOUR "GAME PLAN" IN A POSITIVE DIRECTION.

YOU'LL DISCOVER INTERESTING GOLF TIDBITS THAT WILL BOTH INFORM AND ENCOURAGE YOU. QUOTES FROM WELL-KNOWN GOLFERS WILL GIVE YOU A THOUGHT TO CONSIDER AND MAYBE BRING A SMILE TO YOUR FACE. MEANWHILE, BRIEF SCRIPTURES AND INSPIRATIONAL INSIGHTS WILL HELP YOU SEE MORE CLEARLY THE RELATIONSHIP BETWEEN YOUR GOLF GAME AND THOSE THINGS THAT MATTER MOST IN LIFE.

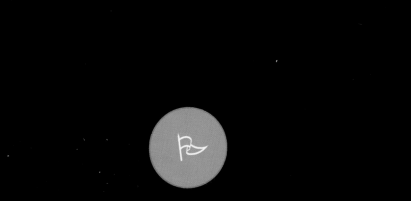

How did I take a twelve?
I had a long putt for an eleven.

THE WEAK BECOME STRONG

You may not be able to change your circumstances, but you——and only you——can change your attitude into that of a winner.

Make it a habit to focus on those thoughts that you believe Christ would have.

BEAT YOUR PLOWSHARES INTO SWORDS,
AND YOUR PRUNINGHOOKS INTO SPEARS:
LET THE WEAK SAY, I AM STRONG.

JOEL 3:10

Bad sausage and five bogeys

will give you a stomachache every time.

MILLER BARBER

My goal this year is basically

to find the fairways.

LAURI PETERSON

NO FEAR

The Lord says that He will be with you. Because of that, you can step

up to the next opportunity with confidence, knowing that regardless

of the outcome, He will be there with you.

FEAR THOU NOT; FOR I AM WITH THEE:

BE NOT DISMAYED; FOR I AM THY GOD:

I WILL STRENGTHEN THEE; YEA, I WILL HELP THEE;

YEA, I WILL UPHOLD THEE

WITH THE RIGHT HAND OF MY RIGHTEOUSNESS.

ISAIAH 41:10

I don't care to join any club
that's prepared to have me as a member.

THE DUES HAVE BEEN PAID

Thankfully, when it comes to being allowed in "God's club," no vote can keep you out and no amount of money is necessary to get in. The price has been paid—in blood, the blood of Jesus Christ. The Lord Jesus paid our dues for us, once and for all; admission is now free to anyone who wants to enter.

HE MADE HIM WHO KNEW NO SIN
TO BE SIN ON OUR BEHALF,
SO THAT WE MIGHT BECOME THE RIGHTEOUSNESS
OF GOD IN HIM.

2 CORINTHIANS 5:21 NAS

*The fun you get from golf
is in direct ratio to the effort
you don't put into it.*

BOB ALLEN

Have you ever noticed what golf spells backwards?

AL BALSKA, AMERICAN WRITER

YOU DESERVE A BREAK

To neglect a weekly day of rest and relaxation will eventually lead to burnout. Remember: Even God rested on the seventh day!

REMEMBER THE SABBATH DAY, TO KEEP IT HOLY.
SIX DAYS SHALT THOU LABOUR,
AND DO ALL THY WORK: BUT THE SEVENTH DAY
IS THE SABBATH
OF THE LORD THY GOD:
IN IT THOU SHALT NOT DO ANY WORK.

EXODUS 20:8-10

I don't need to know where the green is.
Where is the golf course?

THE RIGHT DIRECTION

Of course, the game plan is to keep on the right road, but if you happen toget off, be wise enough to repent and turn around. Keep your alignment squarely on Him. Choose those things that will bring you closer to Him.

REPENT, AND BE BAPTIZED EVERY ONE OF YOU
IN THE NAME OF JESUS CHRIST
FOR THE REMISSION OF SINS,
AND YE SHALL RECEIVE THE GIFT OF THE HOLY GHOST.

ACTS 2:38

When you start
driving your ball down
the middle, you meet a
different class of people.

PHIL HARRIS, COMEDIAN

I've had a good day when
I don't fall out of the cart.

SOME DAYS ARE LIKE THAT!

Guard against getting discouraged when you have bad days. God is still there, and your future with Him is bright.

IN THE DAY OF PROSPERITY BE HAPPY,
BUT IN THE DAY OF ADVERSITY
CONSIDER—GOD HAS MADE THE ONE
AS WELL AS THE OTHER.

ECCLESIASTES 7:14 NAS

In 1996, Bernhard Langer denied that he was quitting the game after being disqualified for signing an incorrect scorecard following the second round of the U.S. Open. Langer said, "I am not a quitter, and I am certainly not a man to run away from my problems."

I guess there is nothing that will get your mind off everything like golf will. I have never been depressed enough to take up the game, but they say you can get so sore at yourself that you forget to hate your enemies.

WILL ROGERS, HUMORIST (1879–1935)

In 1927, Glenna Collett Vare turned down
$50,000 to play golf professionally,
saying she wanted to play for the love
of the game only. Vare, the winner
of six U.S. Women's Amateur championships
between 1922 and 1935, kept her word.

HONESTY IN ALL THINGS

If you compromise your values to succeed, you may win a little but you will lose a lot. Honesty is not the best policy—it's the only policy of which God approves. Make sure your "yes" means "yes," and your "no" means "no."

PRAY FOR US: FOR WE TRUST WE HAVE
A GOOD CONSCIENCE,
IN ALL THINGS WILLING TO LIVE HONESTLY.

HEBREWS 13:18

Water creates a nuerosis in golfers.
The very thought of this harmless fluid
robs them of their normal powers of
rational thought, turns their legs to jelly,
and produces a palsy of the upper limbs.

PETER DOBEREINER, WRITER

YOUR THOUGHTS
MAKE A DIFFERENCE

Attitude does make a difference, doesn't it? And what you focus your thoughts on will make a difference in how you live. Today, choose to think on those things that will improve your performance.

FINALLY, BRETHREN, WHATSOEVER THINGS ARE TRUE,
WHATSOEVER THINGS
ARE HONEST, WHATSOEVER THINGS ARE JUST,
WHATSOEVER THINGS ARE PURE,
WHATSOEVER THINGS ARE LOVELY,
WHATSOEVER THINGS ARE OF GOOD REPORT;
IF THERE BE ANY VIRTUE,
AND IF THERE BE ANY PRAISE, THINK ON THESE THINGS.

PHILIPPIANS 4:8

BEAUTY AND THE BEST

The original course designer is God. Our best efforts to create fabulous, lush environments are a pale reproduction of something He thought up a long time ago. Only a fool would fail to see God's hand in the creation; only a fool would say there is no God.

THE FOOL HATH SAID IN HIS HEART,
THERE IS NO GOD.

PSALM 14:1

TROUBLE SPOTS

Jesus never promised us a pain-free, trouble-free existence on earth. In fact, He warned us that we would, indeed, have trouble. But as we seek Him, the Lord promises to help us through the trouble spots.

GOD IS OUR REFUGE AND STRENGTH,
A VERY PRESENT HELP IN TROUBLE.

PSALM 46:1

Bernhard Langer, a devout Christian,
won the 1985 and 1993 Masters,
but is unfortunately best remembered
for a four-foot putt he missed,
allowing the U.S. to win the Ryder Cup in 1991.

UNDER THE CIRCUMSTANCES

If you are going to conquer your circumstances, let your gaze be on God and your glance on your problems. Focus on Him; to allow your attention to be drawn away from Him will only create more instability. Get in a "zone" with God, and He will help you out from under your circumstances.

A DOUBLE MINDED MAN IS UNSTABLE IN ALL HIS WAYS.

JAMES 1:8

If there is any larceny in a man,
golf will bring it out.

PAUL GALLICO, WRITER (1897—1976)

THE PROS & CONS OF ANGER

When we try to defend our egos, or lash out at another person in anger, we have sinned. In either case, don't carry anger into the next day. Get it out of your system by dealing with it before the sun goes down today.

BE YE ANGRY, AND SIN NOT:
LET NOT THE SUN GO DOWN UPON YOUR WRATH:
NEITHER GIVE PLACE TO THE DEVIL.

EPHESIANS 4:26-27

The friends you make on the golf course
are the friends you make for life.

JESSICA ANDERSON VALENTINE, SCOTTISH GOLFER

KNOWN BY YOUR FRIENDS

Jesus was never reluctant to be among sinners, but He chose to spend most of His time with His disciples. As a rule, our closest friendships are usually with people who share our faith and values. Your friends will have an influence on you.

BLESSED IS THE MAN THAT WALKETH NOT
IN THE COUNSEL OF THE UNGODLY,
NOR STANDETH IN THE WAY OF SINNERS, NOR SITTETH IN
THE SEAT OF THE SCORNFUL. BUT HIS DELIGHT IS
IN THE LAW OF THE LORD;
AND IN HIS LAW DOTH HE MEDITATE DAY AND NIGHT.

PSALM 1:1-2

You can't go into a shop
and buy a good game of golf.

WHEN YOU DON'T GET

WHAT YOU WANT

If you win by deceit, fraud, cheating, lowering the standards, or in anyother improper manner, your success will bring you sadness rather than joy. An honest man plays an honest game and accepts an honest defeat——or enjoys an honest victory.

WHY IS THY SPIRIT SO SAD? . . .

1 KINGS 21:5

A golf ball simply cannot find a hole by itself. Even if it could, the ball would never do so willingly, after the hatred and hammering you've heaped on it to get it to the green.

DICK BROOKS, AMERICAN CARTOONIST

In 1993, at thirty-three years of age
and just three months after winning his first major,
The PGA Championship,
Paul Azinger learned he had bone cancer
in his right shoulder. Less than
a year later, Zinger was welcomed
back to the game—
cancer free—at the Buick Open in Michigan.

ENDINGS & BEGINNINGS

Rest assured that God will have new opportunities for you as you
trust Him and allow Him to direct your paths in the year to come.

TRUST IN THE LORD WITH ALL THINE HEART;
AND LEAN NOT UNTO THINE OWN UNDERSTANDING.
IN ALL THY WAYS ACKNOWLEDGE HIM,
AND HE SHALL DIRECT THY PATHS.

PROVERBS 3:5-6

I deny allegations by Bob Hope

that during my last game I hit an eagle,

a birdie, an elk, and a moose.

GERALD R. FORD,

THIRTY-EIGHTH PRESIDENT OF THE UNITED STATES

Tommy Armour, the "Silver Scot" as he was respectfully known, won the British Open and the U.S. Open, despite having one of his eyes destroyed during World War One in a mustard gas attack. Besides his tournament wins, Armour was one of golf's most successful writers of instructional books.

In 1996, devout Christian,
Tom Lehman, won his first major,
the British Open, and became the
first American ever to win the tourney
at the Royal Lytham and St. Annes course.
In his remarks as he accepted
the Claret Jug, Lehman said,
"I really believe God loves all of us....
I know He cares about me.
I know He cares about you."

FINALLY, BRETHREN, WHOSOEVER THINGS
ARE OF GOOD REPORT,
IF THERE BE ANY VIRTUE,
AND IF THERE BE ANY PRAISE,
THINK ON THESE THINGS.

PHILIPPIANS 4:8

DayMaker
GREETING BOOKS

© 2003 by Barbour Publishing, Inc.

ISBN 1-58660-821-5

Book design by Kevin Keller | designconcepts

Cover photograph © Nora Good/Masterfile

Interior photography © Photonica/p. 8 Nichael Darter, p. 12 Mel Curtis, p. 20 Rieder Photography, p. 24 Erik Rank, p. 42 Anne Menke, p. 50 Peter Zeray

Scripture quotations, unless otherwise noted, are taken from the King James Version of the Bible.

Scripture quotations marked NAS are taken from the New American Standard Bible, © 1960, 1962, 1963, 1968, 1971, 1972, 1973, 1975, 1977 by The Lockman Foundation. Used by permission.

Published by Barbour Publishing, Inc., P.O. Box 719, Uhrichsville, Ohio 44683, www.barbourbooks.com

Member of the
Evangelical Christian
Publishers Association

Printed in China.

5 4 3 2 1

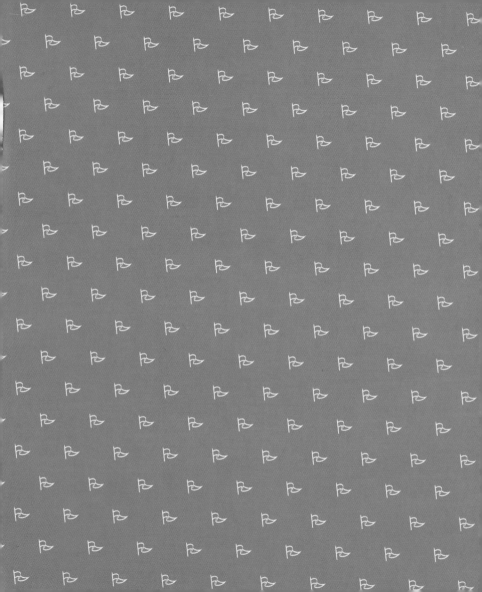